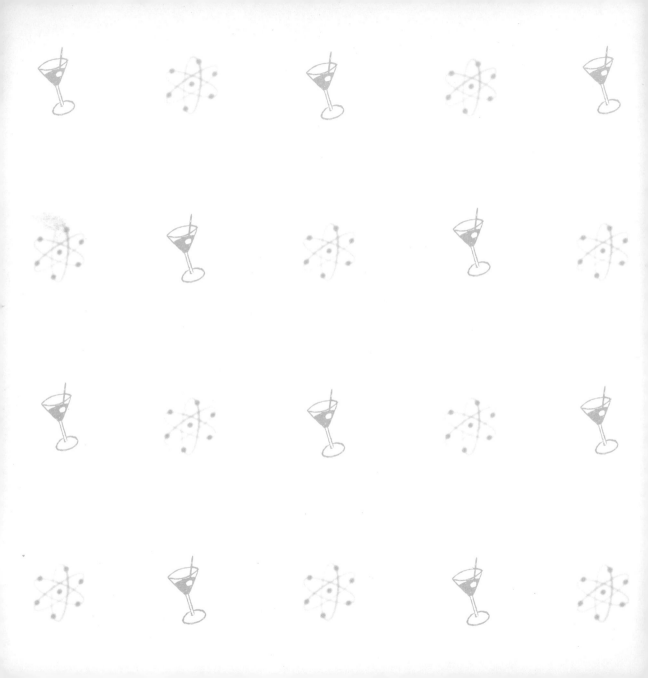

Atomic Cocktails

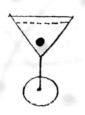

Mixed drinks for modern times

Atomic

Cocktails

Karen Brooks, Gideon Bosker, and Reed Darmon, with Kirsten Pierce

CHRONICLE BOOKS

SAN FRANCISCO

Copyright © 1998 by Karen Brooks and
Gideon Bosker.

Illustration credits:
Photos on pages 34, 50, and 82:
Copyright © Archive Photos
Drawings on pages 2, 3, 35, 44, 49, 67, and
on the cover: Copyright ©1960 Calvert
Distillers Co.

Design by Reed Darmon

Library of Congress Cataloging-in-
Publication Data:

Atomic cocktails: mixed drinks for modern
times/Karen Brooks, Gideon Bosker, and
Reed Darmon.
          p. cm.
Includes index.
ISBN 0-8118-1926-4 (hc)
1. Cocktails. I. Bosker, Gideon. II. Darmon,
Reed. III. Title.
TX951.B7783 1998
641.8'74—dc21   97-34026
               CIP

Printed in Hong Kong

Distributed in Canada by Raincoast Books
8680 Cambie Street
Vancouver, B.C. V6P 6M9

10 9 8 7 6 5 4 3 2

Chronicle Books
85 Second St.
San Francisco, CA 94105

www.chroniclebooks.com

Dedication

To George, who
shook up my life.
— *Karen Brooks*

Contents

Cocktail Nation

No longer slinking,
Respectably drinking,
Like civilized ladies and men,
. . . Cocktails for Two.

from Murder at the Vanities
(song by Arthur Johnston
and Sam Coslow)

SEEING THE TOWN FROM EVERY ANGLE!

From the perspective of a child growing up in the 1950s, cocktails were forbidden, secret potions that put smiles the shape of crescent moons on adult faces of the Ozzie and Harriet generation. Whenever my parents decided to throw a party, mixed drinks were de rigueur — as essential, in fact, as our weekly delivery of milk and Land O' Lakes butter from Chicago's Bowman Dairy. In our house, cocktails meant laughter, dancing, spirited conversations, and getting to stay up late and watch grown-ups act like kids. No wonder I had recurring dreams about cocktails. I remember these dreams as vivid, silent movies of my adolescent imagination: giggling adults telling jokes or convoluted tales as they held pretty glasses filled with colored liquids, all of this seen through the hyper-pink and ultra-blue hues of Technicolor film.

Although lemonade and Bosco were the strongest brews that flowed in my veins during those years, I fell under the spell of cocktail culture at an early age. There was an aura about drinking that my naive mind tried to decipher. The Humphrey Bogart movies, the films by Billy Wilder, the Dean Martin Show, the inebriated antics of Sammy Davis, Jr., and the non-stop weddings and bar mitzvahs at Chicago's Drake Hotel introduced me to elixirs of euphoria at

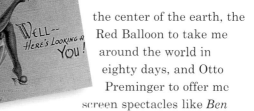

a very young age. I admit it. I was entranced by these precious, carefully prepared drinks in little glasses that made my parents look twinkle-eyed at each other and that fueled uproarious hilarity at my father's Friday night bridge game.

After all, I was an outsider, and having never tasted a martini or screwdriver, I was too young to make the connection between drinks that looked as innocent as water, lemonade, or iced tea — yes, they smelled a bit odd — but that seemed to put my aunts and uncles and grandparents and older cousins in a warm and fuzzy, sweet and light frame of mind. I had the vague sense that cocktails were a kind of magic elixir that took my parents and others of their generation to another, better place, if only for an afternoon or evening. I sensed, too, that cocktails were the dividing line between being a boy and being a man. I had Jules Verne to invite me to

the center of the earth, the Red Balloon to take me around the world in eighty days, and Otto Preminger to offer me screen spectacles like *Ben Hur*. But my parents and James Bond had something else. They had Scotch on the rocks, brandy, sherry, and gin and tonic to tickle their imagination and help them see the world in a calmer and more soothing light.

As was the custom in so many suburban homes, fancy bottles of liquor were displayed in a mahogany cabinet in our living room under lock and key. I remember being very intrigued by the idea of a beverage that did not need refrigeration and that would last for months on end before being consumed. On special occasions, my father unlocked the doors to the cabinet as if they were the secret entrance to a Pharaoh's tomb. He would remove one bottle at a time, carefully study the labels, and position these gleaming testimonials to fine distilling, along with all the necessary accoutrements, on top of the bar in our paneled recreation room. I was fascinated by the dizzying cavalcade of "cocktail furniture," as my father called it, that was arranged for celebratory gatherings of friends and family: the crystal goblets, swizzle sticks, ice cubes, silver shakers, martini olives, paper umbrellas, and maraschino cherries. It was a ritual that, without fail, signaled a party in which high spirits would flow among old friends. It meant an evening of Julie London and Perry Como on the hi-fi, a house filled with guffaws, cackles, and fine pastry, and people from the old country discussing the latest episode of Sid Caesar's *Show of Shows*.

During these parties, I studied the moves — and movies — of my parents' generation, and realized that cocktails were nothing less than magical, mind-altering lubricants for social intercourse.

After the denials of Prohibition, the austerity of the Great Depression, and the deprivation of World War II, Americans uncorked their pent-up craving for alcohol in the 1950s. What resulted was a dreamlike world of perfumed elixirs, of clear, opalescent, amber, pink, and blue concoctions of mixed, straight, shaken, or stirred potions that lowered inhibitions to limbo levels and connected souls through the liquid heat of ethanol and all its iterations.

And with it came the Atomic Cocktail, a good stiff drink with many variations. Although it was a short-lived fad, the Atomic Cocktail was used to elevate the spirits of Americans who were buoyed by postwar optimism, but still made edgy

by the dark cloud of East-West conflict. With time, the prospects for peace improved and the good times rolled. Atomic drinks gave way to high-falutin' cocktails designed to stimulate the palate and prepare the spirit for an America on the rise.

Pluralistic in spirit and politically correct, the cocktail of the fifties became the fuel that powered the engines of industry and commerce. Mixed drinks were revered symbols of business savvy and all-American know-how. The multi-martini lunch catalyzed the deals that turned America into a postwar economic super-power. In the clubby, oak-lined drinking dens of Detroit, New York, and Chicago, the power barons of industry made sure that '57 Chevys, Lucky Strikes, and Fruit of the Loom underwear would become immutable fixtures on Main Street, USA. With drinks in hand, whether on the patio or at the country club, back-slapping good old boys clinked glasses in order to celebrate a more peaceful and prosperous world where rocket ships piercing blue stretches of sky suggested there were no limits to the high

life that awaited the *I Love Lucy* and *The Honeymooners* generation.

Eventually, the cocktail came to represent the unique American talent for combining disparate components into a final product suitable for mass consumption. In fact, some say our culture is a big mixed drink of diverse cultures combined like flavored syrups and spirits and poured into a welcoming cocktail nation.

Whatever layer of cocktail life suits your fancy, we hope this book will take you there. Combining original recipes that capture the spirit of the fifites cocktail with upgraded variations on classic drink recipes, *Atomic Cocktails* will bring you back to the future. It will transport you to a good-times, shake-it-up-baby state of mind where, at least for an hour or two, all appears to be well with the world.

— GIDEON
BOSKER

Gadgets and Gizmos

You don't need a miniature bar to master the art of the cocktail. But you do need the basics, listed below, plus a sharp paring knife, a good corkscrew, and a stash of plastic sword toothpicks.

Bar spoon: This is the classic tool for stirring drinks or muddling ingredients. The best ones are skinny and long-handled, with a twirled

shaft in the middle and small spoon on the end. Do not use with carbonated drinks — the metal is not kind to bubbles.

Blender: This is essential for drinks made with crushed ice. A sturdy model with a powerful motor can double as an ice crusher.

Citrus juicer: An old-fashioned glass reamer or even a plastic one that fits over the rim of a measuring cup will do. But for frequent use or large quantities, an electric squeezer is a dream.

Cocktail shaker: Choose between two styles: the Boston and the standard (or "old style"). The Boston, preferred by bartenders, is a two-piece set including a 16-ounce mixing glass and a slightly larger steel cone that fastens upside-down over the top to create a sealed container for vigorous shaking; you'll also need to buy a separate cocktail strainer. It's not a stylish accessory, but the advantages are quickness and ease of preparation. The more elegant and expensive standard shaker consists of a shell (often of sleek, bulbous chrome) and a tightly fitted top with a built-in strainer in the neck. If you put a premium on visual presentation, this is the ticket.

BAR TALK

Cocktail strainer: Also called a Hawthorne strainer, it's designed with a spring-coil rim that clips snugly over a Boston shaker glass. Use to strain chilled ingredients without ice for a "straight up" drink.

Jigger/pony: This standard metal measuring device is shaped like a tiny hourglass, with a 1½-ounce jigger on one end and a 1-ounce pony on the other.

Mixing pitcher: Look for one made of glass, with a pinched, molded lip that holds back the ice when you pour the drink. Use it for stirring martinis or mixing more than two drinks at a time.

Muddler: A rounded hardwood stick is the classic for mashing sugar and bitters, crushing mint, or cracking ice cubes. For an alternative, use the end of a rolling pin or a ceramic mortar and pestle.

Shot glass: A good device for 1½-ounce measurements, with lines to do the math.

Stirring rod: This glass stick is for stirring martinis or carbonated mixers.

Swizzle sticks: An assortment of stir sticks should be on hand for a fun finishing touch. The gamut runs from campy plastic productions to elegant glass-blown shapes.

11

Glassware Chart

There's an art, ritual, and beauty to serving a cocktail in the right glass. The range of styles is impressive, from hand-blown martini glasses to the masculine architecture of a Pilsner glass to the retro cool of an old shot glass. Many glasses are interchangeable, and part of the fun can be serving a drink in something unexpected.

 Champagne Flute: 6 to 8 ounces

 Highball: 8 to 10 ounces

 Pilsner: 12 to 14 ounces

 Chimney: 10 to 14 ounces

 Irish Coffee: 8 to 10 ounces

 Pousse-Café: 3 to 4 ounces

 Cocktail/ Martini Glass: 4 to 6 ounces

 Large Wine Goblet: 10 to 14 ounces

 Shot Glass: 1 1/2 to 2 ounces

 Collins: 10 to 12 ounces

 Old-fashioned: 8 to 10 ounces

 Sour: 6 ounces

Basic Training
The Essentials of Preparation

❋ Sugar Syrup

This is the best sweetener for drinks that are shaken and strained because it requires no dissolving or mad stirring to incorporate. Just splash it into a cocktail shaker or drink for an excellent, concentrated, easy-to-blend sweetener. It's a cinch to make, taking no more than 5 minutes. The formula can be multiplied or cut in half. If you entertain often, make a large batch and store in a clean, covered glass jar; it will keep for several months when refrigerated. If you don't want to make your own, look for bottled sugar syrup at your local liquor store.

- ¹/₂ cup water
- 1 cup sugar

1. In a small saucepan, bring the water to a boil. Remove from heat and add the sugar. Stir until the sugar is completely dissolved.
2. Set aside to cool completely before using or refrigerating.

Makes 1 cup

❋ Salt Rim

Rub a lime or lemon wedge once around the rim of a glass to moisten it. Pour a few tablespoons of coarse salt on a small plate and shake gently to distribute evenly, or place the salt in a small, wide bowl. Turn the glass upside down and dip the rim in the salt. Gently turn the glass back and forth once to coat the rim, and shake off any excess.

❋ Sugar Rim

Depending on the flavor of the drink, rub a lime, lemon, or orange slice around the rim of a glass to moisten it — or dip the rim in a shallow bowl filled ¹/₄ inch deep with a liqueur. Put a few tablespoons of superfine sugar in a small, wide bowl. Turn the glass upside down and dip the rim in the sugar. Gently turn the glass back and forth once to coat the rim, and shake off any excess. Be sure to use superfine sugar, available at most grocery stores; granulated sugar is simply too coarse.

❋ Lemon Twist

To make the most fragrant twist, use a fresh, unblemished lemon.

Trim off both ends of the lemon and scoop out the pulp, leaving just the peel. With a sharp paring knife, cut the peel lengthwise into skinny strips or "twists." Before serving the drink, hold the twist, exterior side down, over the glass and twist it to squeeze the oil onto the surface of the drink. If the recipe calls for it, run the twist around the rim of the glass. For a more pronounced lemon flavor, drop the twist into the drink.

❋ Lemon Aide

This tangy lemonade is perfect for drinks in need of a lemon infusion. It's also a refreshing drink, and all the better when garnished with fresh raspberries and a lemon twist.

- 2 tablespoons superfine sugar or sugar syrup (see page 14)
- ¼ cup fresh lemon juice
- ¾ cup cold water

1. In a mixing glass, dissolve the sugar or sugar syrup in the lemon juice.
2. Add the water and stir to thoroughly combine. Use as directed, or serve in a glass filled with ice cubes.

Makes 1⅛ cups

❋ Nice Ice

The best ice is made from spring water frozen in trays kept away from other freezer foods, which can carry odors. Tap water, unless it is exceptionally good, is not desirable. Some mavens prefer ice cubes for stirring, shaking, and serving "on the rocks." Others swear by cracked ice, which

WHISKY SOUR
90 CALORIES

GIN RICKEY
90 CALORIES

DRY MAR.
160 ORIES

AQUA SIMPLEX
NO CALORIES

MINT JULEP
80 LORIES

SCOTCH and SOD
80 ALORIES

can be purchased at grocery stores or made by plac-
ing cubes in a clean cotton towel and gently cracking them with a muddler or a tap-icer, a convex
steel weight attached to a long flexible plastic han-
dle. Crushed ice can be made in a powerful electric
blender or manual ice crusher. If you entertain a
lot, consider buying an electric ice crusher.

❋ To Chill a Glass
Fill a glass with crushed ice and water and let it
stand a few minutes. Toss out the contents and
pour the cocktail into the chilled glass. Or, rinse a
glass with cold water and place it in the freezer for
about 7 minutes to chill.

❋ Shaking vs. Stirring
The general rule goes like this: Stir clear drinks
such as martinis, Manhattans and gimlets;
shake drinks with juices, creams, and liqueurs. A
stirred drink has a pristine beauty; a shaken one
is cloudier. Martini drinkers are divided on the
correct technique, and while stirring is the classic
method, a new generation prefers shaking because
it releases the smell of juniper in gin martinis and
adds just a hint of effervescence.

❋ Shake It Up, Baby
The art of shaking is easy to master. Fill a Boston
shaker glass with ice. Turn the steel cone upside
down and fit it snugly over the glass so that it
forms a seal. Grip both ends and shake vigorously
up and down or sideways to blend and chill the
ingredients. Set the shaker down, glass side up.
Push gently but firmly on one side to break the
seal. Remove the glass. Fit a strainer over the cone
and strain the mixture into a serving glass.

Mixer's Measurements
A Chart of Weights and Measures

	US	Metric
Dash	$1/8$ oz	2 ml
Bar spoon	$1/2$ oz	15 ml
1 teaspoon	$1/6$ oz	5 ml
1 tablespoon (3 teaspoons)	$1/2$ oz	15 ml
2 tablespoons (pony)	1 fl oz	30 ml
3 tablespoons (jigger)	$1^1/2$ fl oz	45 ml
$1/4$ cup	2 fl oz	60 ml
$1/3$ cup	3 fl oz	80 ml
$1/2$ cup	4 fl oz	125 ml
$2/3$ cup	5 fl oz	160 ml
$3/4$ cup	6 fl oz	180 ml
1 cup	8 fl oz	250 ml
1 pint	16 fl oz	500 ml
1 quart	32 fl oz	1 l

1 chocolate square = 4 tablespoons grated
1 medium lemon = 3 tablespoons juice
1 medium lime = $1^1/2$ to 2 tablespoons juice
1 medium grapefruit = $2/3$ cup juice
1 medium orange = $1/3$ cup juice

The Continental Piano of HARRY GRUBE at...

Cocktail Time

cocktails
for
two

CROWN RECORDS
FULL COLOR HIGH FIDELITY

LOUIS MARTINELLI AND THE CONTINENTALS

VIK
LX-1076
A "New Orthophonic" High Fidelity Recording
A PRODUCT OF RADIO CORPORATION OF AMERICA

isn't it romantic

LPH-36

9 BEATS TO THE BAR

The Benet Hallberg,
Nisse Engstrom and
Reinhold Svensson Trios

MY HEART BELONGS TO DADDY
GROOVIN' DOCTOR
HONEYSUCKLE ROSE
I GOT IT BAD
DESTINATION MOON
OPUS ON
STARS FELL ON ALABAM
TIME ON MY HAND
I'VE FOUND A NEW BAB
TRE BIRR
PINK ELEPHAN
BEL AN

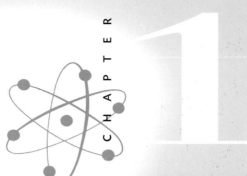

Atomic Cocktails

During the fifties, Russian scientists sent Sputnik up and Hollywood Czars beamed Martians down. Meanwhile, back on Earth, despite the rumblings of rock 'n' roll, society was locked in a bomb shelter of conformity. No wonder we needed nuclear-powered drinks to make sense of it all. With this in mind, these sci-fi selections from our orbiting lab will leave you saying, "Bang, Zoom, Trip to the Moon!"

Rocket Man

Moonshot

Ray Gun

Apricot Fission

Angry Red Planet

Cognac Zoom

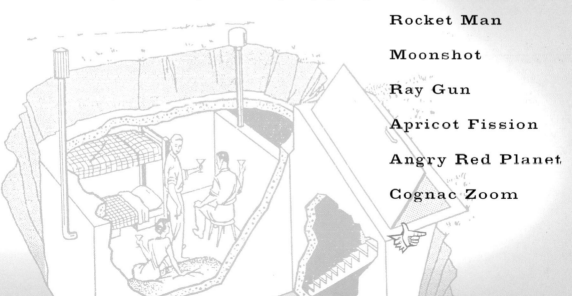

Rocket Man

After a hard day zipping around, taking out death rays and smashing sonic detonators, a guy needs a little flaming cocktail to put it all in perspective. This one is fueled by icy, spicy vodka with a sub-orbital flash of fresh lime. Power ignition comes with a glowing sugar cube that touches down, engulfing the rum-soaked surface with a burst of friendly fire.

- 1 1/2 ounces vodka
- 3/4 ounce Galliano
- 3/4 ounce fresh lime juice
- 1 cup crushed ice
- 1 ounce 151-proof Demerara rum
- 1 sugar cube

1. In a blender, combine the vodka, Galliano, lime juice and crushed ice. Blend until thick and slushy. Pour the mixture into a 6-ounce cocktail glass. Invert a teaspoon over the mixture, tip-end angled slightly down and just touching the side of the glass. Slowly pour 3/4 ounce of the rum over the back of the spoon so that the rum floats on top of the drink. Set aside.

2. Pour the remaining rum into a shot glass. Spear the sugar cube with a bamboo or metal skewer and dip it into the rum to coat.

3. Using a long-stemmed match, and stretching your arms away from your body, carefully light the cube and lay it on top of the rum float to ignite. The flame should be small, but stand back! When the flame dies out, remove the skewer and serve.

Serves 1

Moonshot

The mission here is to ascend skyward on the ethereal vapors of this three-ring cocktail, carefully layered so that each spirit stays in its own stratum. First, pour the booster: a cool buzz of coffee liqueur. Follow with a heat-seeking level of Rumple Minze, a double-whammy peppermint schnapps, and then the bourbon. Toss back in a single firing, and expect an exquisitely prolonged flight. One small sip for man, one giant blast for mankind.

- ½ ounce Kahlúa
- ½ ounce Rumple Minze
- ½ ounce good-quality bourbon

1. Pour the Kahlúa into a shot glass.

2. To create the next layer, invert a teaspoon and place it above the Kahlúa, tip-end angled slightly down and just touching the side of the glass. Slowly pour the Rumple Minze over the back of the spoon so that the liqueur floats on top of the Kahlúa.

3. Repeat the process to create a third layer with the bourbon.

Serves 1

Ray Gun

It doesn't come with a battery or a Captain Video luma-glo card for writing secret messages, but this Ray Gun does carry zap and pop. Shot through with a 25th-century turquoise hue, blasted with spicy orange flavors and interplanetary bubbles, this combo was beamed from the minds of cocktail collectors Jeani Sobotnik and Bruce Bauer.

- 1¹/₂ cups cracked ice or 6 ice cubes
- 2 ounces green Chartreuse
- 1 ounce blue curaçao
- 3 ounces well-chilled Champagne or sparkling wine

1. Fill a cocktail shaker with the ice and add the Chartreuse and blue curaçao. Shake vigorously to blend and chill.

2. Strain the mixture into a Champagne flute or large martini glass. Fill the glass to the top with Champagne or sparkling wine; do not stir. Serve immediately.

Serves 1

Apricot Fission

This drink is a cross between a sour and a fizz, with a strong charge of club soda to detonate the tang of apricot, tangerine, and lemon.

- 1 1/2 cups cracked ice
- 2 ounces apricot brandy
- 1 ounce tangerine juice
- 1 ounce fresh lemon juice
- About 4 or 5 ice cubes
- 1 to 2 ounces chilled club soda

Garnish
- 1 tangerine twist
- 1 fresh mint sprig (optional)

1. Fill a cocktail shaker with the ice and add the brandy, tangerine juice, and lemon juice. Shake vigorously to blend and chill.

2. Fill a 10-ounce glass with the ice cubes. Strain the mixture over the cubes and top with the club soda.

3. Twist the tangerine peel over the top, run it around the rim of the glass, then drop it into the drink. Garnish with a mint sprig, if desired.

Serves 1

Angry Red Planet

Bloody Mary meets Godzilla on Mars in this fiery blend sparked by Asian heat. You can crank up the BTUs by adjusting upward the level of wasabi, a violent green Japanese horseradish paste available at Asian markets.

- Salt rim (see page 14)
- $1/4$ teaspoon grated fresh ginger
- $1/2$ teaspoon wasabi or prepared horseradish
- $1/2$ teaspoon minced garlic
- 4 dashes soy sauce
- 1 tablespoon fresh lemon juice
- Fresh-cracked pepper to taste
- Ice cubes
- 2 ounces pepper vodka
- 3 ounces tomato juice
- 1 teaspoon fresh lime juice
- 1 lime wedge for garnish

1. Salt the rim of a highball glass and chill the glass.

2. Combine the ginger, wasabi or horseradish, garlic, soy sauce, lemon juice, and cracked pepper in a bowl and muddle into a paste (it may be a little lumpy). Stir in the vodka. Pour the mixture into a large mixing glass along with the tomato juice and lime juice.

3. Fill the chilled glass with ice and add the vodka mixture.

4. Garnish with the lime wedge. If desired, stick a chopstick in the glass to use as a stirring rod.

Serves 1

Cognac Zoom

Zooms rocketed to popularity during the forties, the perfect salve for anxious times. This supersonic blend of Cognac, cream, and honey is a soothing antidote for after-work shock syndrome, not to mention the evening news.

- 1 tablespoon honey
- 1 tablespoon boiling water
- 1 1/2 cups cracked ice or 6 ice cubes
- 1 1/2 ounces Cognac
- 1 ounce half-and-half

1. In a cup, dissolve the honey in the boiling water.

2. Fill a cocktail shaker with the ice and add the Cognac, half-and-half, and honey mixture. Shake vigorously to blend and chill.

3. Strain the mixture into a cocktail glass and serve.

Serves 1

VARIATIONS: Add 1/4 ounce crème de cacao for a chocolate undertone. Add 1/4 ounce white crème de menthe for a hint of mint.

Club Paradiso

Our island concoctions are guaranteed to stimulate the neuronal jungle and unleash a cascade of tropical dreams. Luxurious, decadent, rummy, fruity, sexy — we're dealing with serious primal urges here. Can't afford psychotherapy or Club Med? This is the next best option.

Dharma Rum

Mango Margarita

Coconut Lime Rickey

Guava Daiquiri of the Party Gods

Rasta Raspberry Slammer

27

Dharma Rum

If Jack Kerouac and the Beat poets had lived on a tropical island and sipped our decadent cocktail of chocolate, bananas, and rum, they probably would have come up with calypso tunes instead of the dangerous poetry your mother wouldn't let you read. It's a deep, soothing concoction, guaranteed to put a song in your soul.

- 1/2 cup (about 1 small) sliced ripened banana
- 1 ounce crème de banane
- 1 1/2 ounces dark crème de cacao
- 1 ounce dark rum
- 1/4 cup half-and-half
- 1 cup cracked ice

Garnish
- 1 ounce bittersweet chocolate
- 2 maraschino cherries

1. In a blender, combine all the ingredients except the garnishes. Blend at high speed until frothy. Using a small fine-meshed sieve, strain the mixture evenly between two cocktail glasses; discard any remaining chips of ice.

2. To garnish: Using a vegetable peeler or a grater, shave a little bittersweet chocolate over the top of each drink and garnish each with a cherry.

Serves 2

Mango Margarita

Think hot. Think thirsty. Think desperate. Now think satisfaction, as this sensuous drink reaches your lips and cools the throat without chilling your fire. Our formula comes with a tropical aura and a sweet intrigue: a rim dipped in sugar as well as the traditional salt.

- 1/3 cup cubed mango
- 1 1/2 ounces silver tequila
- 1 ounce Triple Sec
- 1/2 ounce fresh lemon juice
- 1 1/2 ounces fresh lime juice
- 1 tablespoon superfine sugar
- 1 1/2 cups cracked ice

Garnish
- 3 tablespoons sea salt
- 3 tablespoons superfine sugar
- 2 lime wedges
- 1 orange slice

1. Puree the mango in a blender. Add the tequila, Triple Sec, lemon juice, lime juice, sugar, and ice, and blend until thick and slushy, with no ice chips remaining.

2. To garnish: Combine the salt and sugar in a wide, shallow bowl. Moisten the rim of a large wine goblet with one of the lime wedges. Dip the rim in the sugar-salt mixture and turn back and forth to coat; shake off any excess.

3. Pour the mango mixture into the prepared glass. Garnish with the remaining lime wedge and the orange slice.

Serves 1

CLOSE COVER BEFORE STRIKING MATCH

Coconut Lime Rickey

This tropical milk shake, with its intoxicating island fragrance, is perfect for languorous sipping on hot summer days. It's simple to master: "You put the lime in the coconut..." and well, you know the rest. The recipe is a specialty at Saucebox, a beachhead of Asian-Island cooking in Portland, Oregon.

- 1½ cups cracked ice or 6 ice cubes
- 1½ ounces light rum
- ½ ounce fresh lime juice
- ¾ ounce coconut syrup (see Note)
- 1 ounce half-and-half
- 1 lime wedge for garnish

1. Fill a cocktail shaker with the ice and add all the ingredients except the lime wedge. Shake vigorously to blend and chill.

2. Strain the mixture into a cocktail glass. Squeeze the lime wedge over the top, then drop it into the drink and serve.

Serves 1

NOTE: Coconut syrup is available at most liquor stores or shops that sell flavored syrups for Italian sodas or specialty coffee drinks.

Guava Daiquiri of the Party Gods

This nectar is a Caribbean carnival, a controlled riot of color, texture, and taste. Instead of the usual crushed ice, this daiquiri is thickened and chilled with piña colada sorbet, creating an ambrosia that will peel the parrots right off your shirt. The proportions below are easily multiplied to delight a crowd of revelers.

- ¼ cup chilled guava juice
- ½ ounce fresh lime juice
- 1½ ounces dark rum
- 1 tablespoon crushed pineapple
- ½ cup Ben & Jerry's Piña Colada Sorbet
- 1 pineapple wedge for garnish (optional)

1. In a blender, combine all the ingredients except the pineapple wedge. Blend until thick and smooth.

2. Pour the mixture into a Collins glass. Garnish, if desired, with the pineapple wedge.

Serves 1

VARIATIONS: Replace half of the piña colada sorbet with blackberry sorbet; garnish with fresh blackberries. Or, experiment with other fruits and sorbets — from chocolate to lemon to strawberry — to create your own fun combos.

Rasta Raspberry Slammer

Okay, mon, just drink de icy, rummy, sweet berry juice. You can do de limbo without it, but we think you go lower wit our cool twist on de daiquiri.

- 1 1/2 cups crushed ice
- 2 1/2 ounces dark Jamaican rum
- 1 ounce fresh lime juice
- 1 ounce pineapple juice
- 2 ounces fresh orange juice
- 1 ounce Cointreau
- 1 cup fresh or frozen unsweetened raspberries
- 1 tablespoon superfine sugar

Garnish
- 2 orange slices
- 2 mint leaves
- 2 firm raspberries

1. Put the ice in a blender and pour in the rum, juices, and Cointreau. Blend for a few seconds, or until the mixture is somewhere between slushy and chunky. Add the raspberries and sugar. Blend for a few seconds, or until well combined and slushy.

2. Divide the mixture between 2 large wine goblets or Collins glasses. To garnish: With a plastic sword toothpick, skewer an orange slice with a mint leaf and raspberry and decorate the rim of the glass.

Serves 2

Martini Madness

The martini is all about manners and ritual, status and mystique, aesthetics and the pursuit of perfection. It's the icon of cocktail culture, glamour in a glass. Perhaps more than any other drink, this classic aperitif has inspired volumes of debate on what constitutes the real thing. Gin or vodka? Shaken or stirred? A modicum of vermouth or a micro-splash? And if you introduce a new ingredient, is it a martini or malpractice? On one end are the hard-core traditionalists, on the other the fanciful expressionists. We offer both the orthodox and reform versions.

The Sacred Truth Martini

Webster's F-Street
Layaway Plan

The Brazen Martini

Left Bank Martini

String of Pearls

Stardust

Perfect! Best Martini I ever tasted!

The Sacred Truth Martini

In the beginning, there was gin and vermouth, stirred over ice and served in a stemmed glass. Simple and swank, punctuated by the elegant architecture of green olives, the martini was a thing of naked beauty. Then came the heretics, who splashed in liqueurs and tinkered with garnishes, and the world has never been the same. This version is our expression of the minimalist camp: gin of the highest order, lean on vermouth, stirred not shaken, and standing on its own integrity.

- 2 pitted green olives
- 1 1/2 teaspoons dry vermouth
- 1 1/2 cups cracked ice
- 3 ounces top-quality gin

1. Spear the olives with a toothpick. Pour the vermouth into a small saucer. Add the olives and turn several times to coat with the vermouth.

2. Fill a cocktail shaker with the ice and add the gin. (Purists say to pour it without making any noise so that you don't bruise the gin.) Stir very gently with a long-handled bar spoon to chill, about 20 revolutions. Or, go the more extreme route and just swirl the gin inside the glass. Either way, work quickly so the ice doesn't melt and dilute the gin.

3. Set the speared olives in a martini glass. Strain the gin over the olives and serve.

Serves 1

36

Webster's F-Street Layaway Plan

This was the martini of choice for F. Scott Fitzgerald, patron saint of the mixed beverage. Could this wild hybrid of good gin and complex Chartreuse be the reason Scott and Zelda were always dancing in those fountains? In any event, the Layaway — a specialty of notorious Bay Area bar master Jamie Reynolds — is best served the way Fitzgerald liked it: day and night.

- ¼ ounce green Chartreuse
- 1½ cups cracked ice or 6 ice cubes
- 2 ounces dry gin
- 1 lemon twist for garnish

1. Chill a martini glass.

2. Pour the Chartreuse into the chilled glass; swirl it around to coat the interior, and discard any excess.

3. Fill a cocktail shaker with the ice and add the gin. Shake vigorously to chill, or use a long-handled bar spoon and stir gently about 20 times. The key is to work quickly so the ice doesn't melt and dilute the gin.

4. Strain the gin into the chilled glass. Garnish with the lemon twist.

Serves 1

The Brazen Martini

Vodka meets violet liqueur in a purple potion that conjures the exotic mystery of wild-flowers and sweet oranges. It's one of those sex goddess drinks, the kind of martini that calls for a lipstick print on the glass, a pair of hot pink maribou slippers, and the sound of "Mondo Mambo" pulsing in the background. The concept sprang from the witty minds behind Brazen Bean, a den of cocktail cool in Portland, Oregon.

- 1 1/2 cups cracked ice or 6 ice cubes
- 2 ounces well-chilled vodka
- 1/3 ounce Parfait Amour (violet liqueur)
- 1 small orange

1. Fill a cocktail shaker with the ice and add the vodka and violet liqueur. Shake vigorously to blend and chill. Strain the mixture into a martini glass.

2. With a vegetable peeler or a very sharp paring knife, cut around the orange continuously to create a thin, 3-inch-long spiral of zest. Drop the spiral in the middle of the drink and serve.

Serves 1

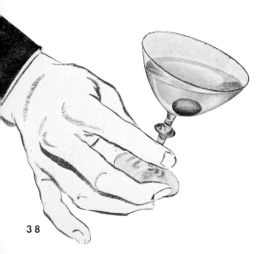

Left Bank Martini

When vodka is infused overnight with fresh rosemary, it takes on the blood-warming tension of cryptic Morse code messages telegraphed across a Parisian bar with the help of flashing eyes. To give this original martini its bohemian scent of herbal dew, you'll need some gauze or cheesecloth. We like to garnish it with big green olives stuffed with goat cheese or feta cheese, and serve it with crusty baguettes on the side.

- 12 ounces vodka
- 3 packed tablespoons fresh rosemary
- 2 ounces dry vermouth
- 1 1/2 cups cracked ice or 6 ice cubes

Garnish
- 4 lemon twists
- 4 rosemary sprigs
- 12 large green olives stuffed with fresh white goat cheese or feta cheese (optional)

1. Pour the vodka into a clean glass pint jar. Crush the rosemary between your fingers and drop it into the jar. Cover tightly and let sit overnight or up to 24 hours at room temperature.

2. Line a strainer with cheesecloth. Strain the rosemary vodka into a pitcher and discard the rosemary. Refrigerate until ready to use.

3. Pour 1/2 ounce of the vermouth into each of 4 cocktail glasses and swirl to coat the sides of the glass; discard any excess.

4. Fill a cocktail shaker with the ice and add the rosemary vodka. Shake vigorously to chill. Strain and divide evenly among the prepared glasses. Garnish each with a lemon twist and rosemary sprig. If desired, spear 3 cheese-stuffed olives on 4 plastic sword toothpicks and set across the glass rim, or serve on the side.

Serves 4

String of Pearls

Think of the following as Grace Kelly, Monaco, white sable, Ella Fitzgerald, and a pink moon in a cocktail glass. It's a pearly post-dinner martini, elegant in its translucence, with white crème de cacao's soft vanilla touch.

- 1¹/₂ cups cracked ice or 6 ice cubes
- 1¹/₂ ounces vodka
- ¹/₂ ounce white crème de cacao
- ¹/₂ ounce half-and-half
- 1 white chocolate kiss

1. Chill a cocktail glass.

2. Fill a cocktail shaker with the ice and add the vodka, crème de cacao, and half-and-half. Shake vigorously to blend and chill.

3. Place the white chocolate kiss in the bottom of the chilled glass. Strain the mixture into the glass and serve.

Serves 1

VARIATION: Add a few splashes of Tia Maria and replace the white chocolate kiss with a chocolate-covered espresso bean.

Stardust

Turn off ESPN, put on Hoagie Carmichael, and turn on the night with this provocative martini for lovers. Sip slowly while gold "stars" twinkle as they arise and drift in your glass. The edible flakes of gold leaf are found in Goldschläger, a cinnamon schnapps liqueur. This recipe is a specialty of Jeani Sobotnik's.

- 1½ cups cracked ice, or 6 ice cubes
- 4 ounces well-chilled vodka
- 1 ounce white crème de cacao
- 2 ounces Goldschläger

1. Chill 2 martini glasses.

2. Fill a cocktail shaker with the ice and add the vodka and white crème de cacao. Shake vigorously to blend and chill.

3. Strain the mixture evenly into the 2 glasses. Float 1 ounce of Goldschläger over the top of each drink. The gold flakes will slowly descend.

Serves 2

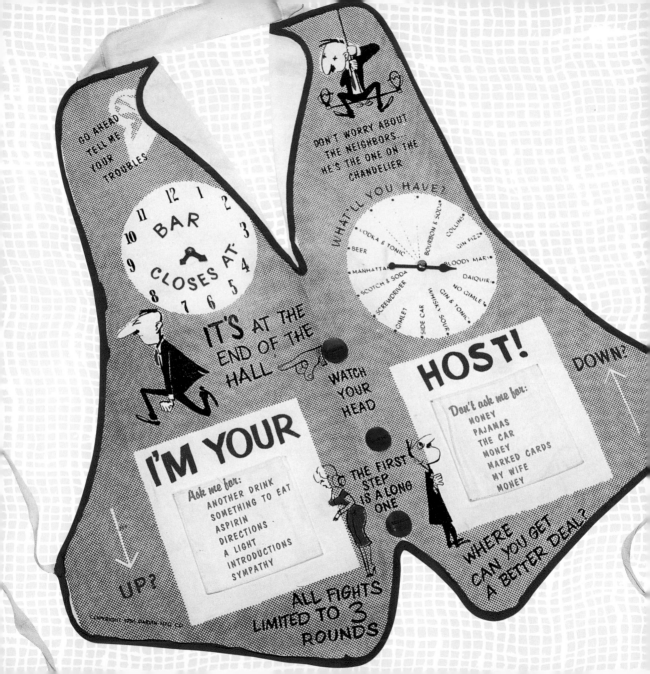

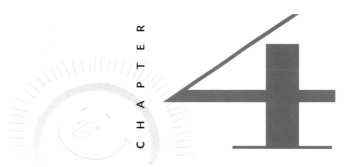

Summer Sizzle

When summer lights a furnace in your throat and the heat makes time stop like a seventh-inning stretch, consider one of our finely tuned temperature-control drinks. Our menu of cool quaffs for hot nights includes fizzes and fruity things, plus a righteous vanilla-orange-vodka shake inspired by that sweet icon of youth, the Creamsicle.

Van Gogh's Anti-Insanity Lemon Tonic

Big Easy Gin Fizz

Chapel of Love

Creamsicle

Neon Watermelon Margarita

Patio Daddy-O Planter's Punch

3 Cool Companions ....when things get hot!

not sweet and heavy
but dry and light

Van Gogh's Anti-Insanity Lemon Tonic

Here's a lemonade beyond the Prozac Zone: brushstrokes of black currant or raspberry liqueur, lemon-hued syrup, see-through vodka, and misty lemonade mingled in a tall glass. Just layering this one brings out the artist in you. Where to serve it? In an endless field of sunflowers on a starry, starry night, of course!

- ½ ounce crème de cassis or Chambord
- ¼ ounce Italian-style lemon syrup (see Note)
- About 5 or 6 ice cubes
- 1½ ounces well-chilled lemon vodka
- ½ cup Lemon Aide (see page 15)

1. Chill a 10-ounce glass.

2. Pour the crème de cassis or Chambord into the bottom of the glass. Add the lemon syrup, but do not stir.

3. Fill the glass to the brim with the ice cubes. Slowly pour in the chilled vodka to create another layer. Then add the Lemon Aide, pouring gently so that the bottom layers remain undisturbed.

4. Serve with a straw and sip from the bottom.

Serves 1

NOTE: Lemon syrup is available at most liquor stores and at shops that sell flavored syrups for Italian sodas or specialty coffee drinks.

Big Easy Gin Fizz

Gin fizzes are usually served in the late morning, when offshore
Louisiana breezes are flavored with musky brine from the bayou and
the languor-inducing heat requires every molecule of energy just to
breathe. A traditional fizz uses lemon and lime juice; ours has both,
plus a taste of orange to transport you to a gumbo dreamland.

- About 9 ice cubes
- 2 ounces gin
- $1/2$ ounce fresh lime juice
- 1 ounce fresh lemon juice
- $1/4$ ounce Cointreau
- $1/2$ ounce sugar syrup (see page 14)
- 2 to 3 ounces chilled club soda

Garnish
- 1 lime wedge
- 1 maraschino cherry
- 1 thin slice lemon peel

1. Chill a highball glass.

2. Fill a cocktail shaker with 6 of the
ice cubes and add the gin, lime
juice, lemon juice, Cointreau, and sugar
syrup. Shake vigorously to blend and chill.

3. Fill the chilled glass with the remaining ice cubes. Strain the mixture into
the glass and add enough club soda to
reach the top. To garnish: With a plastic
sword toothpick, skewer the lime wedge,
cherry, and lemon peel and decorate the
rim of the glass.

Serves 1

Chapel of Love

If you're heading for the altar and need something blissful to keep both sides of the family pain-free during the endless toasts, consider this white sangria summer wedding punch. It's an artful bowl blessed with Spanish magic and citrus effervescence. These ingredients met in the kitchen of our friend Jeani Sobotnik, who suggests exploring different fruit garnishes as the seasons change.

- One 750-ml bottle chilled white Rioja wine
- One 750-ml bottle chilled medium-sweet Reisling wine
- One 750-ml bottle chilled Moscato wine
- 3/4 cup fresh orange juice
- 3/4 cup grapefruit juice
- One 11-ounce bottle chilled Orange Perrier water

Garnishes
- 4 to 8 strawberries
- 1 to 2 star fruit, sliced
- 1 to 2 kiwi fruit, peeled and thinly sliced

1. In a large punch bowl or 2 large pitchers, combine all the ingredients except the garnishes. Refrigerate for at least 1 hour, or until well chilled.

2. Float the garnishes on the top and serve.

Makes 24 four-ounce cups

Creamsicle

Ice cream trucks blaring ricky-ticky music were fixtures of the American summer landscape in the fifties. Like beacons, they charted our way through Ozzie and Harriet suburbs, telling us where to gather for time-tested frozen wonders. That's the memory master mixologist Andy Ricker reconstructed in this homage to the Creamsicle bar, an iconic blend of sweet orange goodness, vanilla intensity, and creamy lightness.

- 1 3/4 cups crushed ice
- 1 1/2 cups cracked ice or 6 ice cubes
- 1 ounce orange vodka
- 1/2 ounce Tuaca
- 2 ounces half-and-half
- 1 teaspoon sugar syrup (see page 14)
- Splash of orange juice

Garnish
- 1 orange slice
- 1 vanilla bean (optional)

1. Fill a 12-ounce glass with the crushed ice.

2. Fill a cocktail shaker with the cracked ice or ice cubes and add all the ingredients except the garnishes. Shake vigorously to blend. Strain the mixture into the glass.

3. Cut a slit in the middle of the orange slice and slide it onto the rim of the glass to garnish. Add a vanilla bean as a swizzle stick, if desired. Serve with a straw.

Serves 1

Neon Watermelon Margarita

It's so hot the fridge is sweating. Mosquitos are dive-bombing, and the overhead fan is turning in slo-mo. You need a break, a heat buster, an off-ramp to icy pink bliss. Our melon margarita, cool and sexy, is the ticket. It's the kind of drink that makes things happen, from back porch barbecues to slow dancing in the living room to Johnny Mathis tunes.

- Sugar rim (see page 14)
- 2¹/₂ ounces silver tequila
- ¹/₂ ounce Triple Sec
- 2 ounces fresh lime juice
- 1 ounce Midori (melon liqueur)
- 2 cups cubed seeded watermelon
- 1 teaspoon superfine sugar
- 1¹/₂ cups crushed ice

Garnish
- Two 2-inch watermelon wedges
- 2 slices kiwi fruit (optional)

1. Sugar the rims of 2 large wine goblets. Set aside.

2. In a blender, whirl the tequila, Triple Sec, lime juice, and Midori. Add the watermelon, sugar, and ice. Blend until the mixture is between slushy and chunky.

3. Divide the mixture evenly between the prepared goblets. To garnish: With a plastic toothpick sword, skewer a watermelon wedge and a kiwi slice and decorate the rim of a goblet; repeat the process to garnish the remaining margarita.

Serves 2

Patio Daddy-O Planter's Punch

Planter's punch is one of those serene drinks to be sipped with reverence and meditation. Some call it a West Indian concoction; others say it is distinctly American, first poured at the Planter's Hotel in St. Louis, circa 1840. And everyone has an opinion on the ratio of sweet-to-sour flavors. Early versions were built around dark rum, lime juice, and sugar syrup. But we like the sunset hues and citrus intrigue of modern versions such as this one, a specialty of Portland food and wine writer Lisa Shara Hall. This recipe easily multiplies to serve in pitchers for a crowd.

- 1 1/2 cups cracked ice or 6 ice cubes
- 4 ounces chilled pineapple juice
- 2 ounces chilled orange juice, preferably freshly squeezed
- 2 ounces chilled fresh lime juice
- 2 ounces dark rum
- Splash of grenadine

Garnish
- One 2-inch pineapple wedge
- 1 maraschino cherry
- 1 orange slice

1. Fill a cocktail shaker with the ice and add the 3 juices and the rum. Shake vigorously to blend and chill.

2. Pour the mixture into a Collins glass. Top with a splash of grenadine. With a plastic toothpick sword, skewer the pineapple wedge, maraschino cherry, and orange slice and decorate the rim of the glass.

Serves 1

The Classics

These are standards of the repertoire, drinks discussed with the kind of reverence usually reserved for retiring baseball legends or deceased heads of state. There's an honesty at work here, and an obsession, an orthodoxy so compelling that purists guard recipes and debate authenticity. Our formulas may not be the last word, but they do deliver the heart and soul of the matter.

Manhattan

Old-Fashioned

Side Car

Whiskey Sour

Gimlet

The Ultimate
Mint Julep

Manhattan

No one agrees on when it was invented, though some legends trace it to the Manhattan Club in the 1870s. And purists can't agree on what goes in it: bourbon, rye, or blended whiskey. And is it equal parts vermouth, or 3 to 1, or 4 to 1? As for bitters, do you reach for Angostura or orange? We reached some conclusions for our bona fide sweet Manhattan. But experiment with proportions and ingredients to craft your vision of the original — or explore the variations below.

How to serve applause-winning MANHATTANS EVERY TIME ...and in just 14 seconds!

- 1 1/2 cups cracked ice or 6 ice cubes
- 1 1/2 ounces bourbon, rye, or blended whiskey
- 1/2 ounce sweet vermouth
- Dash of Angostura bitters
- 1 maraschino cherry for garnish

1. Chill a cocktail glass.

2. Fill a cocktail shaker with the ice and add the bourbon, sweet vermouth, and bitters. Stir with a long-handled bar spoon to blend and chill.

3. Strain the mixture into the chilled glass and garnish with the cherry.

Serves 1

MANHATTAN PERFECT: Add 1/4 ounce dry vermouth and a lemon twist.

DRY MANHATTAN: Eliminate the sweet vermouth; add 1/4 ounce dry vermouth, and garnish with a lemon twist.

ROB ROY: Replace the bourbon with Scotch whisky.

ODDBALL MANHATTANS: Add a few dashes of blue curaçao or green Chartreuse

Old-Fashioned

This may have been the first American cocktail, and it remains one of the greats. Bourbon or blended whiskey usually figures into the format, but Scotch has its own following. Traditionalists don't go for the fizz of club soda, though we think this is a tony touch. But the real secret to success is to muddle the "trimmings" — the lemon twist and orange slice — along with the usual bitters and sugar; the result is a fruity elixir that adds a deeper note to the drink.

- 1 sugar cube, or ½ teaspoon superfine sugar
- 2 to 3 dashes Angostura or orange bitters
- 1½ ounces bourbon, blended whiskey, or Scotch
- 1 lemon twist
- 1 thin orange slice
- 3 or 4 ice cubes
- 2 to 3 ounces club soda
- 1 maraschino cherry for garnish

1. Place the sugar in a 10-ounce old-fashioned glass. Douse it with just enough bitters to coat the cube or soak the sugar.

2. Add the liquor, lemon twist, and orange slice. Using a muddler or something with a blunt end, muddle the mixture until the sugar cube is completely crushed, the juice is extracted from the lemon and orange, and the liquor acquires a pinkish hue.

3. Fill the glass with the ice cubes. Top with club soda. Garnish with the cherry and serve with a swizzle stick.

Serves 1

Side Car

This drink first turned up in Paris as a favorite of Hemingway's crowd of expatriates. It's a wonderful combo of sweet and sour flavors complete with a sugar rim. Think of it as a variation on the classic daiquiri, with brandy in place of rum, and Cointreau instead of sugar syrup. We added a little lemon juice for character and a splash of Rose's lime juice to underline the sweetness. But if you're in a hardcore mood, you can eliminate these two ingredients.

- Sugar rim (see page 14)
- 1 1/2 cups cracked ice or 6 ice cubes
- 1 1/2 ounces good-quality brandy
- 1/2 ounce Cointreau
- 1 tablespoon fresh lime juice
- 2 teaspoons fresh lemon juice
- 1/2 teaspoon Rose's lime juice

1. Sugar the rim of a cocktail glass and chill the glass.

2. Fill a cocktail shaker with the ice and add the brandy, Cointreau, and juices. Shake vigorously to blend and chill.

3. Strain the mixture into the prepared glass and serve.

Serves 1

Whiskey Sour

The great sour formula is built around a triad of flavors: lemon or lime juice, a sweetener, and a liquor. Numerous cocktails take their character from this interplay of sour, sweet, and strong tastes. There's no absolute rule on the ratio of sweet-to-sour, though we like sour as the high note. We also like to use both lemon and lime juice for a richer intensity. And the slushy texture is simply an essential part of the appeal. Traditionally the drink is served in a sour or Delmonico glass, known for its chic, slender shape.

- 1 1/2 ounces bourbon
- 1 tablespoon fresh lime juice
- 1 tablespoon fresh lemon juice
- 1 1/2 teaspoons superfine sugar
- 1 cup crushed ice

Garnish
- 1 orange slice
- 1 maraschino cherry

1. In a blender, combine the bourbon, lime juice, lemon juice, sugar, and crushed ice. Blend until smooth.

2. Pour the mixture into a sour glass. To garnish: With a plastic sword toothpick, skewer the orange slice and cherry and decorate the rim of the glass.

Serves 1

VARIATION: Substitute Scotch, brandy, or amaretto for the bourbon.

Gimlet

In the glory days of the British Empire, officers stationed in the sweaty burgs of New Delhi would invariably take the bite out of a hundred-plus heat wave with this sharp thirst-quencher. And since the Brits exported this classic, the sun has never set on the gimlet. Limeys are quick to remind us that the real goods require candy-sweet Rose's lime juice. But we added a little fresh lime juice, too, for complexity. It's not out of form to experiment with tequila or vodka in place of the gin.

- 1 1/2 cups cracked ice or 6 ice cubes
- 1 1/2 ounces gin
- 1/2 ounce Rose's lime juice
- 2 teaspoons fresh lime juice
- 1 thin lime slice for garnish

1. Chill a martini glass.

2. Fill a cocktail shaker with the ice and add the gin, Rose's lime juice, and fresh lime juice. Shake vigorously to blend and chill.

3. Strain the mixture into the glass. Cut a slit halfway through the lime slice and garnish the rim of the glass.

Serves 1

The Ultimate Mint Julep

A julep is much more than a frosted glass heaped with bourbon and mint sprigs. A real julep is a way of life — one in which ritual and endless debates over the best bourbon are metamorphosed into truth and soul, Southern style. Ours has a deep, heady flavor derived from an overnight infusion of bourbon and mint. The results are as honest as the perfume of a magnolia blossom in a July breeze. We prefer dime-sized mint; as a rule, the smaller the leaves, the sweeter.

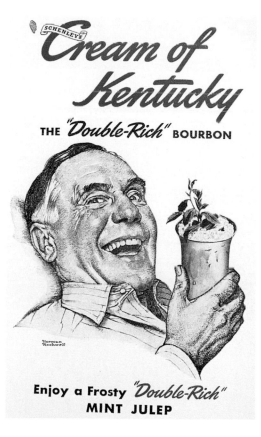

SCHENLEY'S

Cream of Kentucky

THE *"Double-Rich"* BOURBON

Enjoy a Frosty *"Double-Rich"*
MINT JULEP

- 3 cups fresh mint leaves
- 1 bottle (750 ml) Kentucky bourbon
- 1 1/2 to 3 teaspoons sugar syrup (see page 14)
- About 3 cups cracked ice

Garnish
- 6 lemon twists
- 24 fresh mint sprigs

1. Combine the mint leaves and bourbon in a clean 1 1/2-quart jar or glass bowl. Cover and refrigerate overnight.

2. Strain the bourbon into a pitcher; discard the mint. Sweeten to taste with the sugar syrup, adding 1/4 teaspoon at a time.

3. For each serving: Fill a julep cup or Collins glass with the cracked ice. Add 4 ounces of the infused bourbon and stir until the glass frosts (purists hold the glass with a cloth or paper doily, to preserve the frost). Run a lemon twist around the rim of a glass, drop it in, and stir. Pop 4 trimmed mint sprigs into the drink and serve with a short straw. Repeat the process to make the remaining juleps.

Serves 6

Swank, Civil, and Seductive

Here's our recipe for elegant romance by night: candlelight, campy Champagne music, and a collection of chic cocktails to get both of you in the mood. Think strapless rayon cocktail dress and iridescent dinner jacket. Think about a sassy bourbon cocktail with a vanilla-almond perfume, or a sexy aperitif aflame with the juice of blood oranges. Think love at first sip.

Urban Bourbon

Cosmopolitan

Cointreau-A-Go-Go

Roman Holiday

Orange Negroni

Urban Bourbon

Dashiell Hammett meets Sophia Loren: gritty, tried-and-true bourbon seduced by the voluptuous taste of Tuaca, an Italian liqueur that spins the mystery of vanilla, orange, and almond. They come together in our simple composition sparked by a little lemon.

- 1 1/2 cups cracked ice
- 2 ounces good-quality bourbon
- 1/2 ounce Tuaca
- 1 lemon twist for garnish

1. Fill a cocktail shaker with the ice and add the bourbon and Tuaca. With a long-handled bar spoon, stir to blend and chill.

2. Strain the mixture into a cocktail glass. Twist the lemon twist over the top, then drop it into the drink to garnish.

Serves 1

VARIATION: Add a good splash of fresh orange juice to the shaker glass, and shake the mixture vigorously to combine. Serve in a cocktail glass with a sugar rim (see page 14).

Cosmopolitan

Unlike the classics, where the ingredients are all but legally binding, this popular cocktail is open to free expression. A variation on the vodka martini, it has Triple Sec instead of vermouth, along with a big splash of cranberry juice for tartness and rosy hue. But once you get the hang of it, you can play around with cranberry juice substitutes. Try different fruit juices or liqueurs such as Midori (melon) or Parfait Amour (violet).

- 1 1/2 cups cracked ice or 6 ice cubes
- 1 1/2 ounces vodka
- 1/2 ounce Triple Sec
- 1 teaspoon fresh lime juice
- 2 teaspoons fresh lemon juice
- 1 1/2 teaspoons sugar syrup (see page 14)
- Big splash of cranberry juice
- Lime wedge for garnish

1. Fill a cocktail shaker with the ice and add all the ingredients except the lime wedge. Shake vigorously to blend and chill.

2. Strain the mixture into a martini glass. Lightly squeeze the lime wedge over the drink and drop it into the glass to garnish.

Serves 1

Cointreau-A-Go-Go

This pale orange tonic has a nice lemon snap and an even nicer undertone of Cognac. The inspiration comes from bartender and cocktail innovator Nancy Cheek. It's classic and fun, like Donna Reed in go-go boots.

- 1 1/2 cups cracked ice or 6 ice cubes
- 1 ounce Cointreau
- 3/4 ounce Cognac
- 1 tablespoon fresh lemon juice
- Dash of Angostura bitters
- 1 thin lemon slice

1. Fill a cocktail shaker with the ice and add all the ingredients except the lemon slice. Shake vigorously to blend and chill.

2. Strain the mixture into a cocktail glass. Make a slit in the lemon slice and insert it on the rim of the glass as a garnish.

Serves 1

VARIATION: Replace the lemon juice with lime juice and prepare the glass with a sugar rim (see page 14).

Roman Holiday

You don't have to fly off to the Eternal City to indulge in a classy aperitif mingled with Punt e Mes, a frisky bittersweet vermouth with its own spicy aura. Master mixologist Peggy Boston created this orange-scented elixir for Zefiro, an outpost of Mediterranean cool in Portland, Oregon. This Roman Holiday is the quintessential celebration of romance in a glass — very Audrey.

- 1 1/2 cups cracked ice or 6 ice cubes
- 1 1/2 ounces vodka
- 1/2 ounce Punt e Mes
- 1/2 ounce sweet vermouth
- Splash of orange juice
- 1 thin orange slice for garnish

1. Fill a cocktail shaker with the ice and add all the ingredients except the orange slice. Shake vigorously to blend and chill.

2. Strain the mixture into a cocktail glass. Garnish with the orange slice.

Serves 1

Frosty Foursome

GILBEY'S DISTILLED LONDON DRY GIN

"sweet" on whiskey sours?

make your next drink
GREEN RIVER

BLENDED WHISKEY — THE WHISKEY WITHOUT REGRETS

OLDETYME DISTILLERS, INC. Main Office: New York, N.Y.
Distilleries located at Maryland, Kentucky and New Jersey · 75% grain neutral spirits · 90 PROOF

There's pleasure a'plenty on deck—the glass is rising with OLD SUNNY BROOK! Stand by for enjoyment!

Here's to smooth sailing and to smooth-going flavor! Try this fine Kentucky whiskey and see if you've ever taken on a richer cargo.

No sir! This is the best yet! Now I know there are three sides to sailing—the port side, the starboard side and the mellow "Sunny Brook side"!

Orange Negroni

The crimson heat of a blood orange and a hint of sweet orange liqueur create a new mood for the classic Negroni. Very straight, very tart, this drink was originated by cocktail guru Kirsten Pierce. The effect is best described with Pierce's characteristic phrase, *"Oh, yeah!"* If blood oranges are unavailable, substitute navel orange juice.

- 1 teaspoon dry vermouth
- 1 1/2 cups cracked ice or 6 ice cubes
- 1 ounce blood orange juice
- 2 ounces gin
- 1/2 ounce Campari
- 1 1/2 teaspoons Cointreau

1. Pour the vermouth into a cocktail glass. Swirl it about to coat the interior; discard any excess.

2. Fill a cocktail shaker with the ice and add the remaining ingredients. Shake vigorously to blend and chill. Strain the mixture into the glass and serve.

Serves 1

Hot Shots

You don't have to dig a mental trench and hunker down for the winter. When the cold cuts to the bone, celebrate with something from our steamy collection. Pull out your best single-malt Scotch whisky for a wicked hot chocolate, or break out the Jamaican rum and sip to the beat of buttery apple cider. With our mid-winter mixes, you'll be dancing in the snow.

Voodoo Lady

Havana Moon Tea

Chubby Checker Hot Chocolate

Hot Buttered Rumba

Over the Top Shamrock

Eggnog Screamer

Voodoo Lady

Here, Kahlúa and dark rum fall under the spell of Chai concentrate, an exotic Indian black tea blend pungent with sweet spices and honey. Get ready for a jolt of mysterious power, and after consumption stay out of the sunlight and in close touch with friends. This potion was conjured by cocktail creator Houston Davis, who says the magic works best with a fine Barbancourt rum. Look for Chai concentrate in natural food stores or an Indian grocery. An excellent version is made by Tazo (call 1-800-299-9445 for availability in your area). Or make your own black tea concentrate with a few easy steps.

- 1 1/2 ounces dark rum
- 1/2 ounce Kahlúa
- 1/3 cup Chai concentrate (recipe follows)

Garnish
- 2 tablespoons whipped cream
- Ground nutmeg for dusting

1. In an 8-ounce Irish coffee glass or mug, combine the rum and Kahlúa. Set aside.

2. In a small saucepan, heat the Chai concentrate over low heat until steam begins to rise from the surface. Do not boil.

3. Add the concentrate to the rum and Kahlúa. Garnish with whipped cream and a dusting of nutmeg. Serve hot.

Serves 1

CHAI CONCENTRATE: Place 3 Constant Comment tea bags in a teapot. Cover with 2 cups of boiling water and let steep 8 minutes or until dark and richly flavored. Remove the tea bags and stir in 2 tablespoons honey. This yields 2 cups of concentrate, or enough for 5 Voodoo Lady drinks.

Havana Moon Tea

This tea cocktail will transport you to equatorial bliss, no matter how miserable the reality of the elements outside. It evolved from the escapist mind of our friend Ronni Olitsky, a singer and performance artist living in Boston, Massachusetts.

- 1 tablespoon or 1 tea bag orange pekoe tea
- 2/3 cup boiling water
- 2 teaspoons fresh lime juice
- 2 teaspoons packed dark brown sugar
- 1/4 cup Mount Gay rum
- 1 fresh mint sprig

1. Place the loose tea or tea bag in a teapot. Pour in the boiling water and let steep for 5 minutes.

2. Meanwhile, in a small bowl, combine the lime juice, brown sugar, and rum. Stir until the sugar dissolves.

3. Strain the tea into a large mug or an 8-ounce Irish coffee glass. Stir in the rum mixture and add the mint sprig. Serve hot.

Serves 1

Chubby Checker Hot Chocolate

This rich brew, smoky with the bite of single-malt Scotch whisky, will have you twisting the night away. Hot-chocolate artist Lena Lencek created this with Dalwhinnie whisky, which packs a double whammy of Highland heat. If desired, garnish with whipped cream and dark chocolate shavings — or serve with a chocolate swizzle stick. C'mon, baby!

- 3 squares bitter chocolate, chopped
- 2/3 cup water
- 1 cup sugar
- 1/2 teaspoon salt
- 1/4 cup whipping cream
- 6 shots single-malt Scotch whisky
- 5 cups milk

1. Chill the large bowl and beaters of an electric mixer.

2. In a large saucepan, combine the chocolate and water and cook over low heat, stirring constantly, until the chocolate is melted and the mixture is smooth. Add the sugar and salt and stir until the sugar dissolves.

3. Bring the mixture to a simmer and cook until silky and perfectly smooth, with no grains of sugar remaining, about 5 minutes.

4. Meanwhile, in the chilled mixer bowl, beat the cream until soft peaks form.

5. Remove the pan from the heat and let cool slightly, about 3 to 4 minutes. Stir in the whisky. Gently fold in the whipped cream.

6. In a medium saucepan over low heat, scald the milk just until bubbles begin to appear around the edges; do not boil. Remove from the heat and skim off any surface skin if necessary.

7. Pour the chocolate mixture into a heated pitcher or chocolate pot (an elongated teapot). Slowly pour in the scalded milk, stirring well to combine. Serve in 10-ounce Irish coffee glasses or heat-proof mugs.

Serves 6

Hot Buttered Rumba

Forget that pathetic butter raft sent afloat on hot buttered rum drinks. Instead, try our creamed blend of butter, brown sugar, and sweet spices — the mixture mingles with rum and cider the way congos take to marimbas. The effect is even livelier with a side of spicy chicken wings and some hot Afro-Cuban rhythms on the hi-fi.

- 1 teaspoon packed brown sugar
- 1 1/2 teaspoons soft butter
- Pinch *each* of ground cloves, allspice, and cinnamon
- 1/3 cup apple cider
- 1/4 cup dark rum

Garnish
- 2 tablespoons whipped cream
- Ground nutmeg for dusting
- Cinnamon stick for stirring

1. In a small bowl, cream the brown sugar and butter together. Blend in the cloves, allspice, and cinnamon. Put the paste in the bottom of an 8-ounce mug.

2. In a small saucepan, heat the cider until steam rises from the surface; do not boil. Pour the hot cider into the mug and stir vigorously to dissolve the paste. Stir in the rum.

3. Garnish with whipped cream and a dusting of ground nutmeg. Serve with a cinnamon stick for stirring.

Serves 1

Over the Top Shamrock

Here's an original take on Irish coffee: strong brew hidden under a speckled cloud of minted whipped cream and grated chocolate. Created by Tex-Mex king Joe Esparza, this recipe once took Top Irish Coffee honors in a contest in San Francisco. Esparza uses a minimal amount of coffee for a more concentrated kick.

- 1 ounce Baileys Irish Cream
- ½ ounce Bushmills Irish whiskey
- ½ ounce white crème de menthe
- 2 ounces hot strong black coffee

Garnish
- 1½ teaspoons white crème de menthe
- 2 tablespoons whipped cream
- 1 square milk chocolate or bitter-sweet chocolate for grating

1. Combine all the ingredients except the garnishes in an 6-ounce Irish coffee glass or mug.

2. To garnish: Fold the crème de menthe into the whipped cream. Spoon the whipped cream carefully over the drink. Using a cheese grater or vegetable peeler, shave a little chocolate over the cream.

Serves 1

VARIATION: For a St. Pat's Day blowout, add a drop of green crème de menthe to the whipped cream and drizzle a little chocolate sauce on top.

Eggnog Screamer

Warm, creamy eggnog fused with the sweet java tones of Tia Maria is immediately evocative of winter cheer. It's splendid holiday party fare, and our antidote for the season of jangled nerves and credit-card shock syndrome.

- 8 cups (2 quarts) eggnog
- 1 1/4 cups (10 ounces) Tia Maria
- Ground fresh nutmeg for dusting

1. In a large saucepan, heat the eggnog over low heat until steam rises from the surface; do not boil.

2. When the eggnog is hot, remove the pan from the heat and stir in the Tia Maria.

3. Serve in 6-ounce punch cups or heat-proof mugs, garnished with a little nutmeg on top.

Serves 12

In many of the reunions that this holiday season happily brings, Kentucky Tavern—the whiskey that has enjoyed the stewardship of the same family for 75 years—will play its traditional and gracious role.
©1945
Glenmore Distilleries Company, Incorporated,
Louisville, Kentucky

I Love Juicy

Who says drinks in the alcohol-free zone can't be spirited? Our mocktails come with attitude: fun, free-willed, and healthy. We give the basic formulas, but design possibilities expand with every fruit stand and your imagination.

Piña de Nada

E-Man's Lemon Carrot
Chocolate Slide

My Thai

Barbie Blast

Hoolie Coolie
Cantaloupe Cure

Piña de Nada

Here's the best of summer in a glass, a sunny splash of turquoise beaches and laid-back island flavors — the kind of drink that can download your mind for romance, torrid novels, and retro bikini culture. Sure, we've taken the rum out of the piña colada here, but we've left the sun in, adding banana for texture and toasted coconut shreds for fun.

- $^1/_3$ cup chilled coconut cream
- 1 cup chilled pineapple juice
- $^1/_2$ cup crushed pineapple
- $^1/_2$ small very ripe banana, peeled and sliced
- 1$^1/_2$ cups crushed ice

Garnish
- 2 teaspoons toasted coconut shreds
- Two 2-inch pineapple wedges (optional)

1. In a blender, combine the coconut cream, pineapple juice, crushed pineapple, banana, and crushed ice. Blend until thick and slushy.

2. Divide the mixture evenly between 2 large wine goblets. To garnish: Sprinkle the toasted coconut over the top and add a pineapple wedge.

Serves 2

E-Man's Lemon Carrot Chocolate Slide

Willie Wonka meets Bugs Bunny. Here's an avant-garde blend of sweet, spicy, and oh-so-healthy. Titillating taste buds, great night vision: a win-win innovation. The first batch was born in George Eltman's kitchen, a free-form lab of laughter, carrot juice obsession, and ingenuity. The best flavor comes with just-made carrot juice—but most natural food stores offer fresh options, along with Lemon Ginger Echinacea juice, a lemonade with a powerful sting.

- ¼ cup chilled carrot juice
- ¼ cup chopped ripe banana
- ¼ cup chilled Lemon Ginger Echinacea juice
- ¼ square bittersweet chocolate

1. In a blender, whirl the carrot juice, banana, and lemon-ginger juice until thoroughly blended.

2. Pour the mixture into a 10-ounce glass. Grate the chocolate to a fine texture in a spice grinder or with a grater. Sprinkle the chocolate evenly over the top and serve immediately.

Serves 1

My Thai

The kind of flavors found in a Bangkok street market make our exquisite frost-green drink the next best thing to a round-trip ticket to Asia. Like one of those Thai creations exploding a range of vibrant tastes, it's minty and gingery, creamy and lime-perfumed, a little sweet, a little salty, a lot refreshing. Lichee juice, a luscious Asian drink, works wonders here, but experiment with other juices if unavailable. Look for canned rambutan and jackfruit in Asian markets.

เพลินจิตต์

ผมชอบเพลงวอลทซ์ที่สุด โดยฉะเพลง
นี้ มันทำให้ผมต้องเคลิบเคลิ้ม ตกไปสู่
ท้วงค์แห่งความฝันอันแสนหวาน

- 1/3 cup pineapple juice
- 1/4 cup lichee, passion fruit, or mango juice
- 1/4 cup half-and-half
- 2 pieces canned jackfruit
- 2 pieces canned rambutan
- Juice of 1/2 lime
- 2 teaspoons grated fresh ginger
- 1 tablespoon chopped fresh mint
- 1/4 teaspoon salt
- 3 ice cubes

Garnish
- 1 fresh mint sprig
- 1 fresh basil sprig

1. Chill a Collins or Pilsner glass.

2. In a blender, combine all the ingredients except the garnishes and thoroughly blend.

3. Pour the mixture into the chilled glass. Garnish with the mint and basil.

Serves 1

Barbie Blast

Set off by a sugared orange slice, our frosty blend of fresh orange juice and frozen strawberries is beautiful and good for you, too. How else do you expect to become an astronaut, doctor, Olympic gold medalist, CEO, *and* prom queen?

- Sugar rim (see page 14)
- 2/3 cup fresh orange juice
- 2 large frozen strawberries

Garnish
- 2 scant tablespoons superfine sugar
- Orange slice

1. Prepare a large (6-ounce) martini glass with a sugar rim.

2. In a blender, combine the orange juice and strawberries. Blend until thick and smooth. Pour the mixture into the prepared glass.

3. To garnish: Place the superfine sugar in a small saucer. Cut a slit through the center of the orange slice. Dip both sides of the orange slice in the sugar to coat, then slide it onto the rim.

Serves 1

Hoolie Coolie Cantaloupe Cure

Here's our big Rx for jitterbug fatigue, boyfriend blues, and overbuzzed haircuts. It's an easy, ultra-refreshing tonic that relies on top-class ingredients for its charms. We use unfiltered apple juice, quality yogurt (a good, silky goat milk variety is terrific), and a ripe, juicy cantaloupe that exudes summer vitality.

- 1 cup chilled apple juice
- 2 tablespoons plain yogurt
- 1/3 cup cantaloupe chunks
- 2 ice cubes

Garnish
- 1 cantaloupe spear
- 1 fresh mint sprig (optional)

1. Chill a large wine goblet or Pilsner glass.

2. In a blender, whirl the apple juice, yogurt, cantaloupe, and ice cubes until thoroughly combined — a few ice chips may remain.

3. Strain the mixture into the chilled glass. Garnish with the melon spear and mint sprig.

Serves 1

ONE BLOCK NORTH
OF SUNSET BLVD.
BET. SPRING AND BROADWAY

Dancing
'neath the Stars

ASTOR
BAR
HOTEL ASTOR
TIMES SQUARE

Red Room
BAR
MILWAUKEE, WIS.

Mc DONNELL'S
FINE FOOD
and
COCKTAILS

A
Friendly
Place

Where Friends Meet

"TOP OF THE MARK"

DUnkirk 4-3293

VAGABOND'S
HOUSE

2505 WILSHIRE BLVD.
LOS ANGELES

COCKTAILS

The Aloha
Room

CONTINUOUS ENTERTAINMENT

We are Proud of
the Food and Drinks
we serve you.

11502 VENTURA BLVD.
NORTH HOLLYWOOD
CALIFORNIA

SUnset 2-9481

Bar None

These drinks are not exactly off the rack. None of them fits easily into any known slot. Bold, cryptic, esoteric, even frivolous, these are sure bets when you're feeling "been there, drank that."

Mexican Firing Squad

Dada Cocktail

Red Russian

Lady Macbeth

Phive Beta Zappa

83

Mexican Firing Squad

When the Federale asks if you have a last request, this should be it: a drink more potent than a Veracruz sunrise. The liquid fire of tequila is activated with fresh lime, then tamed by the persuasive lull of Kahlúa. If you're taking it without the blindfold, ask for a good pale ale as a chaser.

- 1 ounce good-quality silver tequila
- 1 ½ teaspoons fresh lime juice
- 1 ½ teaspoons Kahlúa
- 1 lime wedge
- 1 glass pale ale (optional)

1. In a shot glass, combine the tequila, lime juice, and Kahlúa.

2. Moisten the rim of the glass with the lime wedge.

3. Drink the entire contents in one shot. Follow with the ale, if you like.

Serves 1

Dada Cocktail

As the Dadaists might say: Let us break down. Let us be good. Let us create a new drink. No=Yes. Dada kicks you in the mind and you like it. So let us challenge your idea of what a rum cocktail can be. The purple haze and black currant undertone of this whimsical cocktail was created by the lovely Kathy Budas for the Portland Institute of Contemporary Art's Dada Ball, a night of thought-provoking decadence on the banks of Oregon's Willamette River.

- 1½ cups cracked ice or 6 ice cubes
- 1½ ounces light Barcardi rum
- 1½ teaspoons fresh lime juice
- 1½ teaspoons crème de cassis
- 1 fresh mint sprig

1. Fill a shaker glass with the ice and add the rum, lime juice, and crème de cassis. Shake vigorously to blend and chill.

2. Strain the mixture into a martini glass. Garnish with the mint sprig.

Serves 1

Red Russian

Our nod to Red Square chic: a drink at once frosty but warm, sparse and pure, with a revolutionary red-orange hue. Drinkers of the world unite—for the Cocktail Party.

- Sugar rim (see page 14)
- 1½ cups cracked ice or 6 ice cubes
- 1½ ounces cranberry vodka
- 1½ teaspoons Cointreau
- 2 ounces fresh blood orange or regular orange juice
- 2 lemon twists for garnish

1. Sugar the rim of a martini glass.

2. Fill a cocktail shaker with the ice and add the vodka, Cointreau, and orange juice. Shake vigorously to blend and chill.

3. Pour the mixture into the prepared glass. Garnish with the 2 lemon twists, crossing one over the other to represent a hammer and sickle.

Serves 1

Lady Macbeth

This Champagne cocktail is a killer, as plush as red velvet, with a woody flavor that flirts with danger. You don't need a high-end Champagne or sparkling wine here, but do consider a good port. The bubbles work here like a mixer, cutting down on the port's thick sweetness and sparking its flavor in mysterious ways.

- 4 ounces chilled Champagne or sparkling wine
- 2 ounces wood-aged ruby port
- 1 lemon twist for garnish

1. Pour the Champagne into a Champagne flute or large wine goblet. Slowly pour in the port, but do not stir.

2. Twist the lemon twist over the top, then drop it in the drink to garnish.

3. Go wash your hands.

Serves 1

Phive Beta Zappa

This is our homage to the pousse-café, an architectural layering of liqueurs originally designed by the French as a "coffee pusher" to chase the post-dinner caffeine. The liqueurs are poured carefully so that each stays in its own colorful stratum. Each sip comes with a different taste exploration, making this the perfect drink for what Jung calls "sensation types."

Once you get a feel for the process, try your own flavors, keeping these things in mind: choose contrasting colors for fun visuals; make sure each layer is lighter than the preceding one to prevent a cave-in; pour very slowly.

- ¼ ounce crème de banane
- ¼ ounce white crème de cacao
- ¼ ounce crème de violette or crème yvette (violet liqueur)
- ¼ ounce cherry brandy
- ¼ ounce heavy (whipping) cream

1. Pour the crème de banane into a shot glass or pousse-café glass.

2. To create the next layer, invert a teaspoon over the crème de banane, tip-end angled slightly down and just touching the side of the glass. Slowly pour the crème de cacao over the back of the spoon so that the liqueur floats on the crème de banane.

3. Repeat the process with the remaining ingredients.

Serves 1

Liqueurs, Liquors, and Bitters:

A Shopper's Guide

Here are the nuts and bolts of Atomic Cocktails, plus a few extras to round out your menu. Our guide comes with recommendations for both the upper and moderate ends of the price spectrum. We encourage using the best quality in any category whenever possible — the difference in results is well worth it. While this list is not exhaustive, it encompasses a range of entertainment options, from the most private encounters to major gatherings.

LIQUORS AND LIQUEURS

Amaretto: The word means "a little bitter" in Italian, and the bitter here is balanced by the characteristic almondlike flavor of sweet, nutty apricot pits. As with most quality imports, the renowned Amaretto Di Saronno is ideal for after-dinner sipping or mixing. Less expensive imitations can be found, but nothing duplicates the taste of this original brand.

Baileys Original Irish Cream: This mocha-flavored liqueur takes its character from Irish whiskey, double cream, coffee, and coconut extract. St. Brendan's produces a less expensive— and some enthusiasts say superior—version.

Brandy: As the oldest and most universal of liqueurs, the world of brandy is vast, complex, and intriguing. The name itself connotes a spirit distilled from wine, but in the larger sense, brandy means liquor distilled from fruit as opposed to that distilled from grain (whiskies), or sugarcane or molasses (rums). Fruit brandies are named for their source, such as apricot brandy or blackberry brandy. And fine brandies come with their own distinctive names, such as Cognac, eau-de-vie, and Armagnac. These are meant to be sipped and savored, but they also can transform a cocktail or hot drink into an elegant adventure. For general mixing purposes, Korbel, E&J, Paul Masson, and Christian Brothers are reliable brands. Metaxa (five- or seven-star) and Cardinal Mendoza are also good for sipping.

Bourbon: Made primarily in Kentucky, this American whiskey is produced from a minimum 51 percent corn mash, then aged in special oak barrels. We recommend the straight bourbons, which have a richer pungency than the blended varieties. Try Basil Hayden's, Maker's Mark, and Knob Creek for straight-out enjoyment or mixing. In the medium price range, Jim Beam or Jack Daniel's will not disappoint. For a special treat, try a fine single-barrel bourbon such as Booker's, Blanton's, or the double-distilled A. H. Hirsch.

Cognac: Named for a region of France where fine grapes are grown, Cognac is known by its amber tones, toasty flavor, and powerful perfume. Generally, quality and price are determined by age, which is signified by stars and letters. The three-star or VS (Very Superior) Cognac, aged up to 5 years, is the least expensive. VSOP (Very Superior Old Pale) Cognac is aged up to 10 years. Napoleon or XO Cognac is aged 15 to 25 years, and the high-end Grande Réserves are aged at least 50 years. Reliable brands are Martell, Rémy Martin, and Delamain. If you can find it, try any Cognac with the Prunier label. Paul Luchère is a popular, moderately priced option.

Chambord: This tony French black raspberry liqueur offers bold amber-ruby color and a thick intensity of sweetness. It's fine for sipping, and blends nicely with vodka in mixed drinks. The budget-minded can substitute a domestic blackberry brandy. Francophiles should try the framboise liqueur by Trimbach.

Chartreuse: Made by French monks at the Carthusian Monastery, this renowned and mysterious brandy-based elixir is produced from a tradition-soaked blend of 130 herbs and spices formulated in secrecy. It comes in two colors: green (a complex herbal liqueur with suggestions of mint and spice) and yellow (sweeter and more mellow, with a lower alcohol content).

Cointreau: Made from the peels of European, African, and Caribbean oranges, this Cognac-based French liqueur has a delicate bittersweet orange heat that hits the back of your throat and says "Hello." It's lovely for after-dinner sipping or mixing.

Crème de banane: Sweet and syrupy, this liqueur has a very distinct banana flavor. Solid brands are Bols and Hiram Walker.

Crème de cassis: Flavored with black currants, this medium-sweet liqueur blends beautifully with vodka, and is de rigueur in the classic Kir drink.

Crème de cacao: This versatile liqueur is thick and syrupy, with a cocoa flavor and vanilla scent. Recipes call for either white or dark versions. There's no difference in taste, so choose a color that suits the drink. Bols and Hiram Walker are two popular brands.

Crème de menthe: This moderately sweet herbal liqueur is made from a variety of mint leaves, but primarily peppermint. The white version is the highest quality; the green version, which is artificially colored, is best used only when color is desired. Bols is a good, moderately priced option.

Curaçao: This potent brandy-based liqueur is made from the peels of green curaçao oranges. It's available in clear, orange, or blue versions, and all three taste the same. Blue curaçao is the most interesting because its color adds an exotic dimension to drinks. Orange curaçao is interchangeable with Triple Sec, though slightly sweeter.

Flavored vodkas: The age-old practice of infusing vodka with fruits, flavorings, or herbs has taken on new life, as vodka flavored with everything from coffee to strawberries turns up in swank cocktails. Absolut Citron (lemon) and the odd-tasting Absolut Kurant (black currant) are wildly popular. Stolichnaya produces an entire line of quality options, including a fiery pepper vodka, an excellent orange vodka, and a lovely lemon vodka. And check out Finlandia's fine cranberry vodka. Or make your own by combining vodka with your favorite ingredient, such as pineapple, cucumbers, or melon. Let the mixture sit in a covered jar at room temperature to mellow for a few days; strain to serve.

Galliano: Bright yellow, with a sweet, complex licorice-vanilla flavor, this Italian herbal liqueur has a touch of bitterness that can add a nice edge to a cocktail. It's a good post-dinner drink, especially after a heavy meal.

Gin: The world is divided into two gin camps: those who love its bracing snap and those who won't touch the stuff. The former group holds that gin is the only choice for the quintessential martini; the latter group is behind the rise of the vodka martini. Martini purists favor London dry gins, known for their floral, aromatic tones and juniper exuberance. Bombay Saffire and Tanqueray are first quality, and Beefeater is a good medium-priced option. For the perfect gin and tonic, try Corney & Barrow, which has just the right bite. American gins tend to be dry, crisp, clean, and more affordable; Seagram's and Gordon's are solid choices. Jenerver, also known as Hollands or Schiedam gin, is for people who really like the taste of gin: It's pungent and almost whiskeylike in flavor. It's not a good mixing gin, it's preferred on the rocks with a slice of lemon as an alternative to a dry martini.

Godiva liqueur: We would be remiss if we didn't tell you about this one: Imagine drinking a candy bar that tastes of bitter orange, with a slight hint of mint and a good chocolate buzz. It's a fun mixer and a decadent dessert cordial. To make a chocolate martini, place 1/4 ounce Godiva liqueur and 2 ounces good-quality vodka in a shaker glass filled with ice; shake to blend and chill, then strain the mixture into a chilled martini glass.

Goldschläger: This Swiss cinnamon schnapps liqueur has particles of gold leaf that float when stirred up, much like a snow dome. If unavailable, substitute Danziger Goldwasser, a brandy-based liqueur with spicy citrus accents. A more affordable equivalent is Bols Gold Strike.

Grand Marnier: An explosion of warm Cognac-orange flavors makes this amber-toned liqueur one of the greats. Fantastic for sipping, it can do wondrous things for the right cocktail. It's an expensive mixer, though, and should be saved for special times.

Irish whiskey: The first Irish whiskey licensed for distillation was Bushmills, back in the 1600s, and it's the only Irish whiskey still manufactured at its original Northern Ireland distillery. It's savored for its gentle, warm nutlike flavor. However, for political and/or taste reasons, some whiskey lovers prefer Jameson. Tullamore Dew is also good for making Irish coffee.

Kahlúa: Sweet and smoky, with a toasted-java flavor, this Mexican liqueur is quite versatile. It's sweeter than Tia Maria and more syrupy, but the two are interchangeable.

Midori: This pale green Japanese liqueur, tasting of sweet, fresh muskmelon, is premier among melon liqueurs. De Kuyper's Melon Liqueur is a good lower-priced alternative.

Parfait Amour: "Perfect love" sums up the way you'll feel about this light, glistening violet elixir from France. The flavor is wonderful and mysterious, an evocation of wildflowers, sweet oranges, and spicy, fruity aromas. If unavailable, substitute crème de violette or crème yvette.

JJ WHISKEY

NOT A DROP IS SOLD TILL IT'S SEVEN YEARS OLD

★ ★ ★

Peppermint schnapps: This intense mint liqueur is more delicate and less sweet than crème de menthe. Rumple Minze, which is 100 proof, is the high end of this spectrum and almost fiery in its peppermint potency. Bols offers a more modestly priced alternative.

Pernod and Ricard: Decendants of the infamous absinthe (a liqueur made with the narcotic wormwood and now banned) and generically known as pastis, these licorice-flavored liqueurs are served neat (without ice) in a tall glass with a side container of ice and a small pitcher of water; water and ice are added to taste.

Port: Originally produced in Portugal, this fortified wine comes in three types: ruby, tawny, and vintage. The color and sweetness of all types change with age and determine the price. The best are at least 15 years old, although there are many delicious non-vintage blends such as Graham's Six Grapes. Typically served as a dessert wine, ports also can be an interesting addition to some drinks. We recommend Fonseca port for quality and affordability.

Rum: Distilled from fermented sugarcane juice or molasses, rum is the darling of the Caribbean.

This essence of rich, warm, earthy flavors is produced in light and dark versions. Light rum, mainly from Puerto Rico and the Virgin Islands, is soft and on the dry side. Dark rum, made primarily in Jamaica, Haiti, and Barbados, is full-bodied; its butter-vanilla flavor is derived from a longer aging process (rum that ages longer than the 3-year standard

takes on a deeper, more complex flavor). Barbencourt and Demerara get our nod for the higher-end brands. Cruzan makes a fine moderately priced light rum; Myers's and Mount Gay produce the equivalent for the dark version. Both dark and light rums can be found in a high-alcohol, or 151-proof version, used for flamed drinks. Another option is Captain Morgan, a vanilla-sweetened rum with a hint of pepper spice—try it for a really different rum and Coke.

Scotch: Many blends are available, all at least 7 years old, like Dewar's or J&B. But the single malts are far more interesting. The range runs from the milder brands of the highlands and lowlands, such as Dalwhinnie, The Macallan, and The Glenlivet, to the funky, peaty richness of the Islay brands, including Laphroaig and Lagavulin. Serve a shot with one cube of ice and a drop of water to bring out the full flavor.

Tequila: This racy Mexican liqueur is made from the blue agave plant. Silver tequila, bottled immediately after distillation, is preferred in margaritas. Gold tequila, aged and more robust, is popular for specialty tequila drinks. Sauza Giro is a solid, moderately priced label, and better than the ubiquitous Jose Cuervos in this range. The high-end options are traditionally served as shots, without lime or salt. Among the top finds are Jose Cuervo Reserve Gold, as smooth as good Cognac; Añejo Tequila Lapiz, which has a fantastic peppery taste; and Porfidio Añejo, which evokes the taste of a good robust wine. Patron Silver is another excellent choice.

Tia Maria: Powered by Jamaican coffee, this rum-based liqueur is drier than Kahlúa and a bit spicier, with its own crisp tang. It's a cordial and more of a sipper than Kahlúa.

Triple Sec: Made with both sweet and bitter oranges, this clear liqueur is interchangeable with Curaçao, though not as sweet. Triple Sec has been called the poor man's Cointreau: a less expensive option.

Tuaca: This lovely brandy-based Italian liqueur has an intriguing flavor with undercurrents of orange, vanilla, and almond. It's delicious for sipping, and versatile for mixing with cocktails or hot cider.

Vermouth: There are two types of vermouth: French, which is dry and pale, with an herbal, nutty flavor that goes beautifully with martinis; and Italian, which is spicy, smooth, and sweeter than the French variety. Martini & Rossi and Cinzano both produce reliable quality vermouths. We also like Punt e Mes, made in Milan and packing a bittersweet complexity of orange and quinine flavors. The result is somewhere between vermouth and Campari, a bitter aperitif. Punt e Mes is fantastic on the rocks or with a splash of soda, and it's intriguing as a mixer.

Vodka: With its waterlike clarity and neutral flavor, vodka is like a blank canvas for the creation of mixed drinks. Though American-made vodkas are good, the best vodkas are usually imports, such as Absolut, Stolichnaya, and Belvedere, which have a very subtle but discernible taste that can elevate a cocktail. A good second-tier choice would be Dutch Ketel One vodka. Among the American options, Skyy is a solid choice. Vodka drinkers usually leave the bottle in the freezer to get the right chill before mixing with other ingredients.

BITTERS

The subject here is not the symbolic Passover bitter herb that clears sinuses and possibly peels paint. These bitters are an

alchemy of botanical exotica and alcohol. With the same evocative powers as Proust's madeleine, they awaken memories of an entire cocktail culture. The flavor of a bitter is so pungent that it can't possibly harmonize with all liquors, but it is so indispensable as a contrasting and catalyzing flavor, that iconic drinks such as the Manhattan and Old-fashioned are lifeless without it. Just a few drops add the lively counterpoint, the elusive nuance, and the exuberance that can turn a good drink into a transcendent one.

Angostura aromatic bitters: If you only buy one kind of bitters, this is the most versatile, with a tart orange flavor and powerful scenting ability.

Campari: This lipstick-red Italian bitter has a quenching quinine flavor. Softer and sweeter than most bitters, it's more popular as an aperitif than a mixer.

Fernet Branca: This intricate, aggressive combination of barks, roots, herbs and spices is used in mixed drinks that need a strong, bitter hit. As an aperitif, it's the finest digestif in the world. A mint version is also available. If you like a sweeter bitter, try Jägermeister.

Orange bitters: Made from the dried peel of bitter Seville oranges, this is less aromatic but fruitier than the Angostura. The best brands are from England, including the excellent Holloway's.

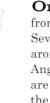

FOR ALL YOUR COCKTAILS

Alphabetical

By Main Alcohol Ingredient

ACKNOWLEDGMENTS

This book was shaken with one part creative juices, one part vintage collectibles and one part sharp editorial insights. We toast the following for sharing their cocktail secrets, cool junk and magnanimous support:

Our dear friend and editor Bill LeBlond, the best in the biz.

Assistant editor Sarah Putman and copy editor Carolyn Miller, two of the top pros around.

Ethel Fleishman, Karen Brooks's collaborator, for being everything a daughter could ask for.

Kirsten Pierce, the infinitely cool cocktail magician, for recipe testing and development, And to her friend Edwardo Gustamante, who did his share of shaking.

Nancy Cheek, bartender extraordinaire, for passing down secrets of the trade.

Ann Wall Frank, the brilliant humorist, for brainstorming and being a great pal.

Jamie Reynolds, the smart, funny bartender of the gods, for pearls of wisdom shot throughout this book.

Jeani Sobotbik, Bruce Bauer, Trent Debord, Samantha Levine, and Pammela Springfield of "Keep 'Em Flying," for sharing their vintage treasures. We are greatly indebted to all of you.

To Michael Butler and the gang at the Uptown Oregon Liquor Control Center, for answering a jillion questions with infinite patience.

To the esteemed bartenders and restaurant owners who generously shared recipes: Bruce Carey, Chris Israel, and Andy Richer of Zefiro and Saucebox; Houston Davis of The Brazen Bean; Jeani Sobotnik and Bruce Bauer of Shaker's Cafe; Joe Esparza of Esparza's Tex-Mex Cafe.

To our friends, for sharing their own fab inventions: George Eltman, Lena Lencek, Lisa Shara Hall, Kristy Edmunds, Kathy Budas, and Ronni Olitsky.

To John Gramsted and Randy Gragg, for insights into the martini myth.

To Tim Sills, for exquisite ideas about language.

To Jon Zimmer, the computer whiz, for all the house calls.

To Joan Strouse, Shirley Kishiyama, Edward Taub, Trink Morimitzu, Peter Leitner, Victoria Frey, Sara Perry, Susan Orlean, Miriam Seger, and Gloria Epstein, for loving support.

And to Gideon Bosker's special friends who have shared a special drink or helped contribute to this book: Gene MacDonald, Mark Christensen, Jack Watson, Jan Norris, and Joanne Day.

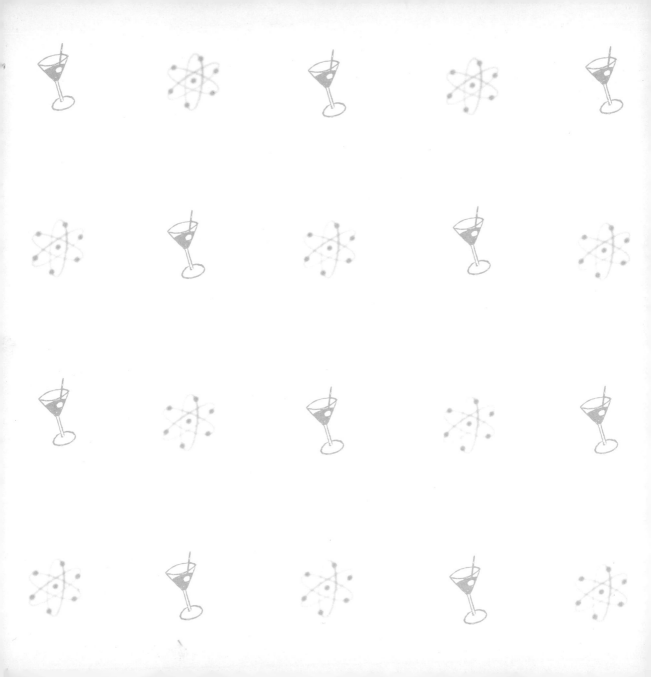